Heartwarming RECIPES for the Busy Cook

To order additional copies of **Heartwarming Recipes for the Busy Cook**
Call 1-800-840-4133 or
visit our web site www.redgold.com

Copyright © 2002
Red Gold, Inc.
P.O. Box 83
Elwood, IN 46036

ISBN: 0-9713817-0-4

Executive Editor: Linda Wallace
Associate Editor: Theresa Warren
Photography: Pavese Imaging, Inc.
Food Styling: Barbara Coad

Designed, Edited, and Manufactured by
Favorite Recipes® Press
an imprint of

FRP

P.O. Box 305142
Nashville, Tennessee 37230
1-800-358-0560

Book Design: Sheri Ferguson
Art Director: Steve Newman
Project Manager: Mary Wilson
Editor: Debbie Van Mol

Manufactured in the United States of America
First Printing: 2002   10,000 copies

TABLE OF CONTENTS

The Red Gold Story

In the 1940s Grover Hutcherson, a retired entrepreneur who had owned and operated thirteen canneries in his lifetime, bought a small cannery in Orestes, Indiana. Electing to forgo retirement he returned to the business he knew so well in order to help supply food to the U.S. Army. In 1942, Hutcherson and his daughter, Frances, founded "Orestes Canning," producing only whole peeled tomatoes and tomato puree. In the early 1970s, Frances and her husband, Ernie Reichart, changed the name of the company to Red Gold and a new "brand" was born. In the 1980s, the Reicharts turned the business over to their children; Brian Reichart, President/CEO, Gary Reichart, Vice-President of Agriculture, and Tina Reichart Anderson, Vice-President of Quality Assurance, Research & Development. Brian's wife, Selita, Vice-President of Employee and Consumer Relations, also joined the family business. The Reichart family continues to lead the company growth by focusing on quality, service, and reinvestment into the business. This once small cannery has now become the nation's largest privately owned tomato processor.

Today, Red Gold, Inc., has three state-of-the-art processing facilities, a 1,000,000 square foot full-service distribution center, and a trucking fleet, RG Transport, all located in central Indiana. Red Gold partners with nearly sixty farmers in Michigan, Ohio, and Indiana to grow Red Gold Tomatoes from proprietary seedlings. Over one hundred different styles and flavors of tomato products are processed for the national, international, and foodservice marketplace. Red Gold Brand products are distributed throughout eleven midwestern states and the southern state of Georgia. The most recent additions to the Red Gold family of products are Redpack and Tuttorosso canned tomato products and Sacramento Tomato Juice. These brands enjoy a strong consumer following in the eastern United States.

The Red Gold brand is advertised in many unique and different ways. These include a 68-foot tall grain silo on I-65 in southern Indiana that resembles a giant can of Red Gold tomatoes; a barn-style Red Gold sign painted on the wall of a local store in Farmland, Indiana; light, humorous television commercials; and a fleet of eighty-five semis displaying a moving billboard of the new Red Gold Tomato design while traveling from coast to coast delivering product.

In the last eight years Red Gold has grown from 170 to over 900 full-time employees. By providing a rewarding, stimulating work environment, Red Gold has been able to attract the type of team members that believe in the work and the product. The continued success of the company will always be directly related to the mission statement, "To Produce the Freshest, Best Tasting Tomato Products in the World."

When I joined Red Gold in 1999 as its first home economist, one of my goals was to provide our busy consumers a new cookbook full of delicious, quick-and-easy recipes that could be prepared in thirty minutes or less.

For the past three years I have been developing recipes with this goal in mind. To ensure success in your kitchen, each recipe was prepared in our test kitchen and taste tested by a panel of consumers. Changes were made to the recipes to reflect the comments conveyed though the consumer's evaluations. Included are more than sixty *Heartwarming Recipes* that proved to be quick, easy and enjoyed by all.

I have always loved cooking and creating exciting new recipes. It has been my pleasure to compile the recipes, hints and helpful tips that appear in this cookbook for you, the *Busy Cook*.

Enjoy!!

Linda Wallace
Red Gold Home Economist

Savory
SKILLET CREATIONS

JIFFY JAMBALAYA

You're only moments away from a Creole adventure when you combine cut-up chicken with rice-and-pasta mix, seasoned tomatoes, and Polish sausage.

SERVINGS
6

PREPARATION TIME
5 minutes

COOKING TIME
25 minutes

1 pound boneless skinless chicken breasts, cut into 1-inch pieces

1 (6.8-ounce) package rice and vermicelli mix with Spanish seasonings

2 cups water

1 (15-ounce) can Red Gold® Crushed Tomatoes with Green Pepper & Mushroom

1/4 teaspoon red pepper

8 ounces cooked Polish or smoked sausage, cut into 1/2-inch slices

- Sauté the chicken in a large skillet coated with nonstick cooking spray over medium-high heat for 3 to 5 minutes or until light brown. Remove the chicken to a platter with a slotted spoon, reserving the pan drippings.
- Reserve the Spanish seasonings packet. Sauté the rice and vermicelli mix in the reserved pan drippings over medium heat until golden brown. Gradually add the water, Red Gold® Crushed Tomatoes with Green Pepper & Mushroom, red pepper and reserved Spanish seasonings, mixing well after each addition. Bring to a boil, stirring occasionally.
- Stir in the chicken and sausage. Simmer, covered, for 15 to 20 minutes or until the liquid is absorbed and the chicken is cooked through, stirring occasionally. For variety, substitute peeled deveined shrimp for the chicken.

Nutritional Facts Per Serving: Cal 340, Fat 13g, Chol 70mg, Sod 1220mg, Carbo 30g, Fiber 1g, Protein 25g, Vitamin A 8%, Vitamin C 25%, Calcium 4%, Iron 15%

 JAMBALAYA
Jambalaya is one of the great classic one-pot dishes of the Louisiana kitchen. The name "jambalaya" comes from the French and Spanish words for ham. With rice as its base, jambalaya is a direct descendent of paella, the Spanish rice dish that usually features several varieties of seafood, chicken, and sausage.

OPEN-FACE OMELET

Bring the flavor of breakfast to dinner. This yummy omelet disappears quickly, so be prepared to make several to keep up with the demand.

6 tablespoons butter

3 cups frozen hash brown potatoes

1/2 teaspoon celery salt

6 eggs

1/4 cup milk

Salt and pepper to taste

1/4 cup chopped green onions

1 (14.5-ounce) can Red Gold® Diced Tomatoes Mexican Fiesta or Red Gold® Diced Tomatoes & Green Chilies, drained

1 cup (4 ounces) shredded Cheddar and Monterey Jack cheese blend

1 tablespoon bacon bits

EGG STORAGE

Do not transfer eggs from their carton to the plastic storage tray in the refrigerator. The thin eggshells are permeable and can absorb refrigerator odors. So keep eggs in the carton they come in. The carton acts as an odor barrier and saves the step of transferring the eggs to the plastic storage tray.

- Melt 3 tablespoons of the butter in a skillet over medium heat. Arrange the hash brown potatoes in an even layer in the skillet. Sprinkle with the celery salt. Cook for 10 minutes or until light brown, turning frequently. Remove the potatoes to a platter. Cover to keep warm.
- Whisk the eggs, milk, salt and pepper in a bowl. Melt remaining 3 tablespoons butter in the same skillet. Add the egg mixture, tilting the skillet to ensure even coverage. Cook, lifting the edge of the omelet as the eggs set to allow the uncooked egg to flow underneath; do not stir.
- Spoon the potatoes evenly over the omelet. Top with green onions, Red Gold® Diced Tomatoes Mexican Fiesta, cheese and bacon bits. Cut into wedges and serve immediately.

Nutritional Facts Per Serving: Cal 240, Fat 17g, Chol 195mg, Sod 760mg, Carbo 13g, Fiber 1g, Protein 9g, Vitamin A 20%, Vitamin C 8%, Calcium 10%, Iron 6%

CHEESE TORTELLINI AND VEGETABLES

Crisp fresh asparagus and cheese tortellini with a creamy sauce are the basis for this one-dish dinner.

1 1/2 cups coarsely chopped fresh asparagus or fresh green bean pieces
1 1/2 cups thinly sliced red bell pepper
1 (14.5-ounce) can Red Gold® Diced Tomatoes or
Red Gold® Diced Tomatoes Roasted Garlic & Onion, drained
2 tablespoons butter
3 tablespoons minced fresh chives
1 tablespoon basil leaves, crushed
1 (9-ounce) package fresh cheese tortellini, cooked, drained
1 1/2 cups cottage cheese
1/3 cup grated Parmesan cheese
Freshly ground pepper

TASTY TURKEY SOUP

Wondering what to do with leftover turkey from the holiday? Create a full-flavored soup by heating together 2 cups diced cooked turkey, 2 cups cooked vegetables, two 14.5 ounce cans Red Gold® Diced Tomatoes Mexican Fiesta, 2 cups water, 1 teaspoon Italian seasoning and 1/4 teaspoon onion powder. If desired, stir in 1 cup cooked pasta or barley and heat through.

- Cook the asparagus, red bell pepper and Red Gold® Diced Tomatoes in the butter in a large skillet until tender, stirring frequently. Stir in the chives and basil.
- Add the pasta, cottage cheese and Parmesan cheese to the asparagus mixture and toss to mix. Serve with freshly ground pepper.
- **Note:** Chopped green tops of scallions can be used in place of chopped fresh chives. Complete the meal with a fresh fruit salad and dinner rolls.

Nutritional Facts Per Serving: Cal 260, Fat 11g, Chol 50mg, Sod 570mg, Carbo 26g, Fiber 3g, Protein 16g, Vitamin A 60%, Vitamin C 130%, Calcium 20%, Iron 10%

ITALIAN SAUSAGE SKILLET

SERVINGS
8

PREPARATION TIME
15 minutes

COOKING TIME
20 minutes

When trying to squeeze in a fast family meal between your job and the activities of your always-on-the-go children, choose this convenient and satisfying recipe.

1 1/4 pounds Italian sausage links, cut into 1/4-inch slices
3 small zucchini or yellow summer squash, chopped
1/2 cup chopped onion
1 (14.5-ounce) can Red Gold® Stewed Tomatoes

DID YOU KNOW?

According to the U.S. government reports on vegetable consumption, tomatoes place second.

If you eat three tomatoes, you will have eaten enough to reach the daily recommended dietary allowance of vitamin C.

There are only thirty-five calories in one tomato.

- Brown the sausage on both sides in a skillet over medium heat. Stir in the zucchini and onion. Cook for 2 minutes, stirring constantly. Add the undrained Red Gold® Stewed Tomatoes and mix well. Reduce the heat to low.
- Simmer, covered, for 10 to 15 minutes or until the zucchini is tender, stirring occasionally. Serve over hot cooked rice or pasta. Substitute chopped red or green bell pepper and chopped green onions for the zucchini if desired.
- **Note:** Yellow summer squash, also called crookneck squash, has a thin edible skin and tender seeds, much like zucchini. Either may be used in this quick-and-easy skillet meal.

Nutritional Facts Per Serving: Cal 290, Fat 17g, Chol 55mg, Sod 560mg, Carbo 20g, Fiber 2g, Protein 13g, Vitamin A 20%, Vitamin C 45%, Calcium 4%, Iron 10%

SKILLET PARMESAN SENSATION

SERVINGS
8

PREPARATION TIME
10 minutes

COOKING TIME
10 minutes

A great recipe to warm your soul on a cold day. Your favorite chicken along with pasta and mixed veggies makes a great one-skillet meal.

1 (9-ounce) package fresh cheese tortellini
1 (6-ounce) package flavor of choice prepared chicken strips, cut into bite-size pieces
1 (10-ounce) package frozen mixed vegetables
2 (15-ounce) cans Red Gold® Crushed Tomatoes with Green Pepper & Mushroom
Salt and pepper to taste
1 cup (4 ounces) grated Parmesan cheese

SASSY SKILLET SUPPER

This four-ingredient recipe makes a mouth-watering main dish in next to no time. In a large skillet brown 1 pound of lean ground beef or pork; drain. Stir in one 14.5-ounce can Red Gold® Stewed Tomatoes, undrained; one 8-ounce can whole kernel corn, undrained; and one package of oriental noodles with pork flavor. Break up the noodles. Simmer, covered, for 10 minutes or until noodles are tender and liquid is absorbed. Makes 4 servings

- Cook the pasta using package directions; drain. Combine the chicken, mixed vegetables and Red Gold® Crushed Tomatoes with Green Pepper & Mushroom, salt and pepper in a skillet and mix well. Bring to a boil; reduce the heat to low.
- Simmer for 3 to 4 minutes, stirring occasionally. Stir in the pasta and sprinkle with the cheese. Simmer just until the cheese melts, stirring frequently.
- **Note:** When saving leftovers that contain tomato products or other foods that stain plastic containers, first coat the container with nonstick cooking spray. It keeps them looking like new.

Nutritional Facts Per Serving: Cal 250, Fat 7g, Chol 40mg, Sod 1300mg, Carbo 29g, Fiber 2g, Protein 17g, Vitamin A 25%, Vitamin C 30%, Calcium 25%, Iron 10%

SOUTHWESTERN SKILLET

SERVINGS
6

PREPARATION TIME
10 minutes

COOKING TIME
10 minutes

Shout olé for an easy one-dish meal the whole family will love.

1 (6-ounce) package prepared chicken strips, cut into 1-inch pieces
1 (16-ounce) package frozen corn, broccoli and red pepper
1 (15-ounce) can black beans, drained, rinsed
1 (15-ounce) can Red Gold® Crushed Tomatoes with
   Green Pepper & Mushroom
2 cups coarsely crushed tortilla chips
1 cup (4 ounces) shredded Cheddar cheese

GIVING
LEFTOVERS
A LIFT

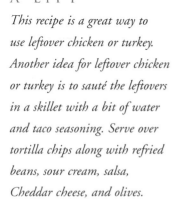

This recipe is a great way to use leftover chicken or turkey. Another idea for leftover chicken or turkey is to sauté the leftovers in a skillet with a bit of water and taco seasoning. Serve over tortilla chips along with refried beans, sour cream, salsa, Cheddar cheese, and olives.

- Combine the chicken, frozen vegetables, black beans and Red Gold® Crushed Tomatoes with Green Pepper & Mushroom in a 10-inch skillet and mix well. Cook, covered, over medium heat for 6 to 8 minutes or until the vegetables are crisp-tender, stirring occasionally.
- Sprinkle the tortilla chips and cheese over the top. Cook, covered, for 2 minutes longer or until the cheese melts. Serve immediately.
- **Note:** Use your favorite frozen vegetable combination. Crush the tortilla chips neatly and easily by placing them in a plastic bag and crushing with a rolling pin.

Nutritional Facts Per Serving: Cal 310, Fat 13g, Chol 25mg, Sod 820mg, Carbo 35g, Fiber 3g, Protein 13g, Vitamin A 15%, Vitamin C 15%, Calcium 15%, Iron 8%

14

GARDEN-STYLE FRITTATA

SERVINGS
6

PREPARATION TIME
15 minutes

COOKING TIME
10 minutes

Great for last minute Sunday brunch! Quick and easy. You can even cut the frittata into small portions and serve as finger food.

8 eggs

1/2 cup (2 ounces) finely grated Romano cheese

7 fresh sage leaves, thinly shredded

1/2 teaspoon salt

1/2 teaspoon pepper

1 tablespoon olive oil

6 medium scallions with tops, thinly sliced

2 (14.5-ounce) cans Red Gold® Diced Tomatoes Mexican Fiesta, drained

 FRITTATA
A frittata is the Italian version of an omelet. It is cooked slowly over low heat. The ingredients are mixed into the eggs and it is served round and unfolded. Frittatas are quick and simple to prepare, with a texture firmer than that of omelets. They are usually made with many of the same ingredients as an omelet. When served with a crisp salad and crusty bread, they make an ideal impromptu meal.

- Beat the eggs in a bowl with a fork just until blended. Stir in the cheese, sage, salt and pepper. Heat the olive oil in a medium nonstick ovenproof skillet over medium heat. Reserve 1 tablespoon of the scallions. Add the remaining scallions to the hot skillet.
- Cook for 2 minutes or until limp, stirring frequently. Add the egg mixture, tilting the skillet to ensure even coverage. Reduce the heat to low. Cook for 3 minutes, lifting the edge of the frittata with a wooden spoon to allow the uncooked egg to flow underneath; do not stir.
- Spoon the Red Gold® Diced Tomatoes Mexican Fiesta over the top of the frittata. Cook for 2 to 3 minutes or just until the eggs begin to set. Sprinkle with the reserved scallions. Broil for 1 to 2 minutes or until set and light brown.

Nutritional Facts Per Serving: Cal 200, Fat 12g, Chol 290mg, Sod 670mg, Carbo 10g, Fiber 3g, Protein 13g, Vitamin A 30%, Vitamin C 15%, Calcium 20%, Iron 20%

CLASSIC SPANISH RICE

SERVINGS
8

PREPARATION TIME
20 minutes

COOKING TIME
45 minutes

Take a quick trip to the sunny Southwest with our Classic Spanish Rice! *Long grain rice paired with delicious Red Gold® products bursts with flavor when combined with chopped onion and green bell pepper.*

8 slices bacon

3/4 cup uncooked long grain
    white rice

1 medium onion, chopped

1 small green bell pepper,
    chopped

1 pound ground round

1 1/2 cups Red Gold® Tomato Juice

1 (15-ounce) can Red Gold®
    Crushed Tomatoes

1/2 cup Red Gold® Chili Sauce

1 tablespoon brown sugar

1 teaspoon salt

1/2 teaspoon pepper

1/2 teaspoon Worcestershire sauce

FIRE AND RICE

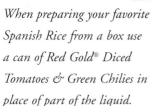

When preparing your favorite Spanish Rice from a box use a can of Red Gold® Diced Tomatoes & Green Chilies in place of part of the liquid.

- Cook the bacon in a skillet until crisp. Remove to a platter using a slotted spoon. Drain the skillet, reserving half the bacon drippings.
- Cook the rice in the reserved bacon drippings until brown, stirring constantly. Add the onion and green bell pepper. Cook until the vegetables are tender, stirring frequently. Transfer to a large saucepan.
- Brown the ground round in the skillet, stirring until crumbly; drain. Stir into the rice mixture. Stir in the Red Gold® Tomato Juice, Red Gold® Crushed Tomatoes, Red Gold® Chili Sauce, brown sugar, salt, pepper and Worcestershire sauce and mix well. Simmer, covered, for 45 minutes, stirring occasionally. Crumble the bacon and sprinkle over the top of the rice just before serving.

Nutritional Facts Per Serving: Cal 280, Fat 10g, Chol 40mg, Sod 920mg, Carbo 28g, Protein 16g, Vitamin A 20%, Vitamin C 45%, Calcium 2%, Iron 15%

CHICKEN PARMESAN RISOTTO

SERVINGS
6

PREPARATION TIME
5 minutes

COOKING TIME
10 minutes

This recipe is quick and easy and can be prepared in one skillet.
The Italian-style risotto has a wonderful chicken flavor.

1 (10-ounce) can cream of chicken soup

1 1/2 cups milk

1/4 cup grated Parmesan cheese

1 (14.5-ounce) can Red Gold® Diced Tomatoes Italian

1 (6-ounce) package Italian-style chicken breast strips, cut into 2-inch pieces

2 cups instant white rice

 LYCOPENE
Recent scientific research indicates that lycopene, a nutrient found in canned tomatoes, is a potent antioxidant and may reduce the risk of heart disease and certain cancers. There is more lycopene in canned tomatoes than in an equivalent amount of fresh tomatoes. The processing of tomatoes extracts lycopene so that it can be easily absorbed into the body. As few as eight ounces of Red Gold® Tomato or Vegetable Juice consumed daily increases lycopene levels in only two weeks.

- Combine the soup, milk, cheese, undrained Red Gold® Diced Tomatoes Italian and chicken in a large skillet and mix well. Bring to a boil. Stir in the rice.
- Cook, covered, over low heat for 5 minutes. Remove from heat. Let stand for 10 minutes or until the rice is tender; stir.

Nutritional Facts Per Serving: Cal 270, Fat 8g, Chol 30mg, Sod 920mg, Carbo 35g, Fiber 1g, Protein 14g, Vitamin A 15%, Vitamin C 10%, Calcium 20%, Iron 10%

TOMATO BASIL CHICKEN

SERVINGS
4

PREPARATION TIME
5 minutes

COOKING TIME
20 minutes

Fresh basil and juicy Red Gold® tomatoes, ripened by the sun, star in this one-dish meal.

DICED
TOMATO
VARIATIONS

Did you know that there are seven diced tomato varieties?
Red Gold® Diced Tomatoes
Red Gold® Diced Tomatoes
  Italian
Red Gold® Diced Tomatoes
  Mexican Fiesta
Red Gold® Diced Tomatoes &
  Green Chilies
Red Gold® Diced Tomatoes
  Chili Ready
Red Gold® Diced Tomatoes
  Chili Ready with Onion
Red Gold® Diced Tomatoes
  Roasted Garlic & Onion
On the next visit to your supermarket, pick up a new Red Gold® diced tomato variety.

2 cups cooked chicken breast strips
1 (14.5-ounce) can Red Gold® Diced Tomatoes Italian
1 1/4 cups water
1 (6-ounce) package rice pilaf mix
1/4 cup fresh basil, chopped
1 tablespoon olive oil

■ Combine the chicken, undrained Red Gold® Diced Tomatoes Italian, water, rice mix, basil and olive oil in a nonstick skillet and mix well.
■ Bring to a boil; reduce the heat to low. Simmer for 15 to 18 minutes or until the liquid is absorbed and the rice is tender, stirring occasionally.
■ **Note:** About 1 1/4 pounds of boneless chicken breasts can be substituted for a 2- to 3-pound broiler/fryer chicken. Twelve ounces or 3/4 pound of boneless skinless chicken breasts equals about 2 cups of chopped cooked chicken.

Nutritional Facts Per Serving: Cal 170, Fat 5g, Chol 20mg, Sod 640mg, Carbo 21g, Fiber 1g, Protein 8g, Vitamin A 10%, Vitamin C 10%, Calcium 6%, Iron 8%

SPRING RAVIOLI

SERVINGS
8

PREPARATION TIME
10 minutes

COOKING TIME
8 minutes

The addition of "fresh from the garden" green beans, basil pesto and grated lemon zest gives this recipe the fresh flavor of spring.

2 teaspoons vegetable oil

1 cup fresh green beans, cut into 1 1/2-inch pieces

1 small yellow bell pepper, cut into 1/2-inch pieces

1 (14.5-ounce) can Red Gold® Diced Tomatoes Italian

1/2 teaspoon salt

1 (16-ounce) package fresh cheese ravioli

1/2 cup sour cream

3 tablespoons basil pesto

2 teaspoons grated lemon zest

- Heat the oil in a large skillet over medium heat. Add the green beans and yellow bell pepper and mix well. Cook for 5 minutes or until crisp-tender, stirring frequently. Stir in the undrained Red Gold® Diced Tomatoes Italian and salt. Cook for 3 minutes, stirring occasionally.
- Cook the pasta using package directions; drain. Combine the sour cream, pesto and lemon zest in a bowl and mix well. Add the pasta and sour cream mixture to the green bean mixture and toss to mix.
- **Note:** Sprinkle ravioli with shredded Parmesan cheese for added flavor. You can use 4 ounces of asparagus cut into 1-inch pieces and 4 ounces of snap pea pods instead of green beans. Add wedges of melon, clusters of grapes and garlic breadsticks to quickly round out this colorful meal.

Nutritional Facts Per Serving: Cal 180, Fat 10g, Chol 20mg, Sod 580mg, Carbo 18g, Fiber 2g, Protein 6g, Vitamin A 15%, Vitamin C 90%, Calcium 10%, Iron 8%

Enjoy
THE PASTABILITIES

TACO PASTA SOUP

Your family will love this quick and convenient but healthy and interesting soup. People find it hard to believe the soup has not simmered all day, as the flavors blend beautifully.

SERVINGS
8

PREPARATION TIME
15 minutes

COOKING TIME
15 minutes

1 pound ground round

1 (46-ounce) can Red Gold® Tomato Juice

1 (15.5-ounce) can Red Gold® Chili Hot Beans

1 (14.5-ounce) can Red Gold® Diced Tomatoes Mexican Fiesta

1 (14.5-ounce) can whole kernel corn, drained

8 ounces rotini

1 envelope taco seasoning mix

1 cup (4 ounces) shredded Cheddar cheese

- Brown the ground round in a stockpot, stirring until crumbly; drain. Add the Red Gold® Tomato Juice, Red Gold® Chili Hot Beans, undrained Red Gold® Diced Tomatoes Mexican Fiesta, corn, pasta and seasoning mix and mix well.
- Cook over medium-high heat until the pasta is tender, stirring occasionally. Ladle into soup bowls. Sprinkle with the cheese.
- **Note:** This recipe can use Red Gold® Diced Tomatoes for a mild flavor, Red Gold® Diced Tomatoes Mexican Fiesta for a medium flavor or Red Gold® Diced Tomatoes & Green Chilies for a hot flavor.

Nutritional Facts Per Serving: Cal 320, Fat 10g, Chol 40mg, Sod 900mg, Carbo 36g, Fiber 5g, Protein 18g, Vitamin A 20%, Vitamin C 60%, Calcium 10%, Iron 15%

TOMATO JUICE TRIVIA

In the United States, 95 percent of all tomato juice is made from concentrate, but all Red Gold® Tomato Juice is made from fresh tomatoes. Our tomato juice is also certified kosher.

MEXICAN PASTA SALAD

SERVINGS
16

PREPARATION TIME
30 minutes

This salad is always a big hit at buffets and especially, picnics. The amount of mayonnaise used allows the salad a longer storage time than that of the traditional pasta salad. If prepared in advance, store in the refrigerator. Just before serving, add one to two tablespoons of milk for a creamier consistency.

Creamy Cilantro Dressing

1/4 cup fresh cilantro, chopped

1/4 cup mayonnaise

1/4 cup sour cream

1 teaspoon salt

Salad

1 1/3 cups (9 ounces) orzo or rosamarina

2 (14.5-ounce) cans Red Gold® Diced Tomatoes Mexican Fiesta, drained

1 (14.5-ounce) can whole kernel corn, drained

1 (15-ounce) can black beans, drained, rinsed

1 cup (4 ounces) shredded Mexican cheese blend

1 cup chopped green bell pepper

2 green onions, thinly sliced

ORZO

The Italian translation for orzo is "barley," but orzo actually is a small rice-shaped pasta. A great rice substitute, orzo works well in soups, stews, pilafs, side dishes, oven bakes, and salads.

- For the dressing, combine the cilantro, mayonnaise, sour cream and salt in a bowl and mix well.
- For the salad, cook the pasta using package directions. Drain and rinse with cold water to cool; drain. Combine the pasta, Red Gold® Diced Tomatoes Mexican Fiesta, corn, black beans, cheese, green bell pepper and green onions in a bowl and mix gently. Add the dressing and toss to coat. Spoon into a lettuce-lined bowl.

Nutritional Facts Per Serving: Cal 160, Fat 6g, Chol 10mg, Sod 460mg, Carbo 22g, Fiber 2g, Protein 5g, Vitamin A 10%, Vitamin C 20%, Calcium 6%, Iron 8%

PASTA CLUB SALAD

SERVINGS
6

PREPARATION TIME
10 minutes

REFRIGERATION TIME
1 hour

No pasta salad with a taste this superb is easier to prepare! This recipe uses already cooked and prepared chicken and a pasta salad mix.

1 (10.4-ounce) package classic ranch with bacon pasta salad
1 (6-ounce) package prepared chicken strips, flavor of choice
1 (14.5-ounce) can Red Gold® Diced Tomatoes, drained
¼ cup sliced green onions

- Prepare the pasta salad using package directions. Drain the pasta.
- Stir in the chicken, Red Gold® Diced Tomatoes and green onions. Chill, covered, for 1 hour before serving.
- **Note:** The prepared chicken strips can be found in the deli meat section of your grocery. They are completely grilled and ready to eat.

Nutritional Facts Per Serving: Cal 260, Fat 1g, Chol 0mg, Sod 330mg, Carbo 25g, Fiber 1g, Protein 5g, Vitamin A 15%, Vitamin C 4%, Calcium 2%, Iron 8%

 SAVE ON PREP TIME

Green peppers are purchased by 84 percent of all consumers, primarily for flavoring purposes. Now customers can save time with this new, value-added product. Red Gold® Crushed Tomatoes with Green Pepper & Mushroom can be used in multiple ways, such as over pasta, on baked potatoes, or in a favorite dish.

TORTELLINI VEGETABLE SALAD

SERVINGS
4

PREPARATION TIME
20 minutes

*Experience a taste of summer with this delicious garden salad.
The flavors are delightful.*

9 ounces fresh cheese tortellini

2 (14.5-ounce) cans Red Gold® Diced Tomatoes, drained

1 (12-ounce) package mixed greens

1 1/2 cups sliced fresh mushrooms

1/2 cup garlic onion vinaigrette

1/2 cup toasted garlic onion croutons

10-MINUTE MEAL

*Feeling hurried in the kitchen?
Take a deep breath and count
to ten . . . then sit down to a
relaxing meal of Red Gold®
Diced Tomatoes with Roasted
Garlic & Onion heated and
poured over cooked pasta. Add
a tossed salad and garlic bread
and your meal is on the table
in ten minutes.*

- Cook the pasta using package directions. Drain and rinse with cold water; drain.
- Combine the pasta, Red Gold® Diced Tomatoes, mixed greens and mushrooms in a salad bowl and mix gently. Add the vinaigrette and toss to coat. Sprinkle with the croutons.
- **Note:** When Red Gold® Diced Tomatoes are used as a replacement for fresh tomatoes, they must be drained, rinsed with cold water and drained again. This will remove the excess juice and leave beautiful fresh-diced tomatoes for use in a garden salad or a recipe.

Nutritional Facts Per Serving: Cal 190, Fat 7g, Chol 20mg, Sod 420mg, Carbo 26g, Fiber 2g, Protein 5g, Vitamin A 8%, Vitamin C 10%, Calcium 6%, Iron 8%

ITALIAN TOMATO PASTA BAKE

SERVINGS
8

PREPARATION TIME
10 minutes

BAKING TIME
25 minutes

Great evening meal for the family on the go. Cook the pasta one day in advance, and in a few minutes you will have a one-dish meal ready for the oven.

3 cups (8 ounces) penne
1 pound ground round
3 (15-ounce) cans Red Gold® Crushed Tomatoes
with Green Pepper & Mushroom
1/2 teaspoon basil
1/2 teaspoon salt
2 cups (8 ounces) shredded Italian blend cheese

PASTA SAUCE SUBSTITUTION

Red Gold® Crushed Tomatoes with Green Pepper & Mushroom is a new product that can be found on your grocer's shelf next to the Red Gold® Crushed Tomatoes. The product can be used in place of spaghetti sauce. Boil your pasta and combine with heated Red Gold® Crushed Tomatoes with Green Pepper & Mushroom, sprinkle with Parmesan cheese, and you have a meal in minutes.

- Preheat the oven to 350°F. Cook the pasta using package directions; drain. Cover to keep warm.
- Spray a 13×9-inch microwave-safe baking dish with nonstick cooking spray. Microwave the ground round in the prepared dish until brown and crumbly, stirring occasionally; drain. Stir in the Red Gold® Crushed Tomatoes with Green Pepper & Mushroom, basil and salt.
- Microwave until the mixture comes to a boil. Stir in the pasta. Bake, covered, for 15 minutes. Sprinkle with the cheese. Bake for 5 to 10 minutes longer or until the cheese melts. Serve with a mixed green salad.

Nutritional Facts Per Serving: Cal 340, Fat 14g, Chol 55mg, Sod 640mg, Carbo 31g, Fiber 3g, Protein 21g, Vitamin A 25%, Vitamin C 8%, Calcium 10%, Iron 20%

SOUTHWESTERN BAKED PASTA

SERVINGS
8

PREPARATION TIME
20 minutes

BAKING TIME
30 minutes

When you want to cook once and eat twice, prepare this pasta and cheese dish. The beauty of this Southwest version is that you can reheat leftovers in the microwave.

8 ounces rotini or your favorite pasta

1 (14.5-ounce) can Red Gold® Diced Tomatoes & Green Chilies or any other variety of Red Gold® Diced Tomatoes

1 (10.5-ounce) can Cheddar cheese soup

2 cups (8 ounces) shredded processed American cheese

1/4 cup low-fat milk

1/4 cup sliced green onions

1 teaspoon chili powder

1 cup crushed tortilla chips

10-MINUTE PASTA DISH

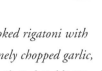

Toss hot cooked rigatoni with olive oil, finely chopped garlic, chopped basil, Red Gold® Diced Tomatoes (drained), and cubed Brie cheese.

- Preheat the oven to 375°F. Cook the pasta using package directions; drain. Combine the undrained Red Gold® Diced Tomatoes & Green Chilies, soup, 1 cup of the cheese, milk, green onions and chili powder in a bowl and mix well. Add the pasta and toss to mix.
- Spoon the pasta mixture into a 13×9-inch baking dish. Sprinkle with the remaining 1 cup cheese. Bake for 20 minutes. Sprinkle with the tortilla chips. Bake for 5 to 10 minutes longer or until light brown.
- **Note:** Must have meat? To vary this recipe, stir about 1 cup of cubed fully cooked ham into this can-do-quick oven meal.

Nutritional Facts Per Serving: Cal 330, Fat 14g, Chol 35mg, Sod 870mg, Carbo 36g, Fiber 2g, Protein 13g, Vitamin A 30%, Vitamin C 6%, Calcium 25%, Iron 10%

PENNE PASTA TOSS

Boneless chicken and green beans make a delicious and low-fat pairing in this Mexican tomato sauce. Use your favorite shaped pasta...penne and shells work well.

SERVINGS
6

PREPARATION TIME
10 minutes

COOKING TIME
10 minutes

1 cup penne
2 (14.5-ounce) cans Red Gold® Diced Tomatoes Mexican Fiesta
1 (14.5-ounce) can green beans, drained
1 (14.5-ounce) can lima beans, drained
1 (6-ounce) package prepared chicken breasts, chopped
1 cup (4 ounces) shredded mozzarella cheese

 CANNED FOOD NUTRITIOUS?

You bet! In fact, canned vegetables are equally as nutritious as, or more nutritious than, their fresh counterparts. Once canned, a product usually maintains its nutrient levels, even after one to two years. This is important, since canned products are harvested at the peak of ripeness and usually canned within only a few hours, sealing in the nutrients. Fresh vegetables often are picked before their nutrient content has peaked and spend seven to fourteen days in transit. Unlike many fresh items, canned products are available year-round at peak quality.

- Cook the pasta using package directions; drain. Combine the undrained Red Gold® Diced Tomatoes Mexican Fiesta, green beans and lima beans in a large skillet and mix well. Bring to a boil, stirring occasionally.
- Add the pasta and chicken to the bean mixture and mix well. Cook for 5 minutes or until heated through, stirring occasionally. Sprinkle with the cheese. Serve immediately.
- **Note:** Use cooked Italian sausage in place of chicken and Red Gold® Diced Tomatoes Italian to give this pasta toss an Italian flair instead of a Mexican flair. Also try using other canned vegetables of your choosing, such as Italian-style green beans.

Nutritional Facts Per Serving: Cal 180, Fat 3.5g, Chol 20mg, Sod 760mg, Carbo 24g, Fiber 4g, Protein 14g, Vitamin A 20%, Vitamin C 15%, Calcium 10%, Iron 15%

SAVORY PORK AND PASTA

SERVINGS
6

PREPARATION TIME
10 minutes

COOKING TIME
10 minutes

This is a quick meal for the busy family. The only prior preparation is to ensure the ground pork is not frozen; fresh is best.

1 1/2 cups (4 ounces) fusilli, penne or other small pasta

1 pound ground pork

1 onion, chopped

1 teaspoon basil

1 teaspoon salt

1/2 teaspoon pepper

1 (14.5-ounce) can Red Gold® Stewed Tomatoes

1 (8-ounce) can Red Gold® Tomato Sauce

1 zucchini or yellow squash, chopped

STICKY PASTA

The secret to evenly cooking pasta that does not stick together is a large pot of continuously boiling water. Use a pot large enough for the pasta to move around freely and keep the water boiling.

- Cook the pasta using package directions; drain. Cover to keep warm. Heat a nonstick skillet over medium-high heat. Add the ground pork and onion. Cook until the ground pork is brown and crumbly, stirring frequently; drain. Stir in the basil, salt and pepper. Add the undrained Red Gold® Stewed Tomatoes and Red Gold® Tomato Sauce and mix well. Bring to a boil; reduce heat to low.
- Simmer for 5 minutes, stirring occasionally. Add the pasta and zucchini and mix well. Cook for 2 to 5 minutes or until heated through, stirring occasionally. Serve with a crisp green salad topped with Red Gold® Diced Tomatoes and French bread.

Nutritional Facts Per Serving: Cal 280, Fat 12g, Chol 50mg, Sod 750mg, Carbo 25g, Fiber 3g, Protein 17g, Vitamin A 15%, Vitamin C 25%, Calcium 6%, Iron 15%

SONORA-STYLE SPAGHETTI

SERVINGS
8

PREPARATION TIME
10 minutes

BAKING TIME
30 minutes

Use leftover chicken or turkey from the family dinner for this colorful, taste-satisfying spaghetti dish.

7 ounces spaghetti

1 small onion, chopped

1 tablespoon butter

1 (15-ounce) can Red Gold® Crushed Tomatoes
with Green Pepper & Mushroom

1 (14.5-ounce) can Red Gold® Diced Tomatoes & Green Chilies

2 cups (8 ounces) shredded processed American cheese

Salt and pepper to taste

2 cups chopped cooked chicken or turkey

- Preheat the oven to 350°F. Cook the spaghetti using package directions; drain. Sauté the onion in the butter in a large skillet until tender. Stir in the Red Gold® Crushed Tomatoes with Green Pepper & Mushroom, undrained Red Gold® Diced Tomatoes & Green Chilies, cheese, salt and pepper.
- Cook until the cheese melts, stirring frequently. Stir in the spaghetti and chicken. Spoon the spaghetti mixture into a 13×9-inch baking dish sprayed with nonstick cooking spray. Bake for 30 minutes or until bubbly. Optional: Garnish with sliced jalapeños.
- If you are vegetarian, you could omit the chicken or turkey.

Nutritional Facts Per Serving: Cal 300, Fat 13g, Chol 60mg, Sod 1460mg, Carbo 27g, Fiber 2g, Protein 20g, Vitamin A 20%, Vitamin C 20%, Calcium 20%, Iron 10%

 MILDER FLAVOR?

If you want a milder flavor, use Red Gold® Diced Tomatoes Mexican Fiesta instead of Red Gold® Diced Tomatoes & Green Chilies. Also, use sliced green onions on top of the casserole instead of jalapeño peppers.

Rush Hour
DINNERS

CHEESY POTATO DINNER

SERVINGS
8

PREPARATION TIME
5 minutes

COOKING TIME
12 minutes

As the saying goes, March comes in like a lion and goes out like a lamb. Give winter its last hurrah with a cozy family dinner served around the fireplace. This one-dish meal makes it easy.

1 pound ground round or boneless skinless chicken breasts, cut into bite-size pieces

1 (16-ounce) package frozen bite-size shredded seasoned potatoes

1 (14.5-ounce) can Red Gold® Diced Tomatoes Mexican Fiesta

1 (8-ounce) jar processed cheese sauce

- Place the ground round in a microwave-safe dish. Microwave until brown, stirring occasionally; drain. Add the potatoes, undrained Red Gold® Diced Tomatoes Mexican Fiesta and cheese sauce and mix well.
- Microwave on High for 10 to 12 minutes, rotating and stirring after 6 minutes.
- If using prepared chicken, combine all of the ingredients in a microwave-safe dish and microwave on High for 10 to 12 minutes.

Nutritional Facts Per Serving: Cal 200, Fat 10g, Chol 30mg, Sod 960mg, Carbo 17g, Fiber 2g, Protein 11g, Vitamin A 10%, Vitamin C 10%, Calcium 15%, Iron 6%

MEXICAN FIESTA

Research shows that Mexican flavor–enhanced products are among the most purchased variety. Red Gold® responded to this research by introducing a diced tomato product with cumin and lime juice. Red Gold® Diced Tomatoes Mexican Fiesta is the perfect cooking solution for the consumer desiring a mild heat of zesty flavor. The product has multiple uses, such as over pasta, over baked chicken, or in a favorite Mexican dish.

COOL CHICKEN WRAPS

Celebrate the Fourth of July in style with a light supper featuring this tasty wrap. Enjoy at home or pack in your cooler along with some fresh fruit and a cool beverage and you are set for an evening of fun.

MAKES
8 wraps

PREPARATION TIME
10 minutes

4 (12-inch) flour tortillas

1/2 cup mayonnaise

1/2 teaspoon dill weed

4 cups shredded lettuce or cabbage

2 (6-ounce) cans water-pack chicken or tuna, drained, flaked

1 (14.5-ounce) can Red Gold® Diced Tomatoes, drained, rinsed

1/4 cup chopped green onions

1 cup (4 ounces) finely shredded Cheddar cheese

- Spread 2 tablespoons of the mayonnaise on one side of each tortilla and sprinkle with dill weed. Layer equal amounts of the lettuce, chicken, Red Gold® Diced Tomatoes, green onions and cheese in the center of each tortilla.
- Fold the bottom of each tortilla up 2 inches and then roll to enclose the filling. Wrap each tortilla tightly with plastic wrap.
- Store in the refrigerator until serving time. Cut each wrap into halves before serving.

Nutritional Facts Per Wrap: Cal 270, Fat 18g, Chol 45mg, Sod 470mg, Carbo 14g, Fiber 2g, Protein 13g, Vitamin A 6%, Vitamin C 4%, Calcium 10%, Iron 6%

 KEEP YOUR LETTUCE CRISP!

Keep your lettuce wrapped in a paper towel and in a plastic bag in the refrigerator and it will stay as fresh as when you bought it.

BREAKFAST BURRITOS

Have a hard time getting out of bed? Wake up to something new . . . breakfast burritos. This tasty recipe can help you jump start your morning.

1 pound ground round
1 pound ground sausage
6 potatoes, cooked, peeled, chopped or sliced
1 (14.5-ounce) can Red Gold® Diced Tomatoes & Green Chilies

6 eggs, beaten
1 (14-ounce) package 10-inch flour tortillas
1 cup (4 ounces) shredded Cheddar cheese
1 1/4 cups Red Gold® Salsa

HANDY DICED TOMATOES

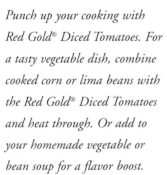

Punch up your cooking with Red Gold® Diced Tomatoes. For a tasty vegetable dish, combine cooked corn or lima beans with the Red Gold® Diced Tomatoes and heat through. Or add to your homemade vegetable or bean soup for a flavor boost.

- Brown the ground round and sausage in a skillet, stirring until crumbly; drain. Add the potatoes and mix well. Cook until the potatoes are brown, stirring frequently. Stir in the undrained Red Gold® Diced Tomatoes & Green Chilies and eggs. Simmer for 10 minutes, stirring occasionally.
- Microwave the tortillas in batches on a paper towel for 15 seconds or until warm. Spoon 1/2 cup of the ground round mixture onto the center of each tortilla. Top each with an equal portion of the cheese and 2 tablespoons Red Gold® Salsa. Fold the bottom of each tortilla up approximately 2 inches and roll to enclose the filling. Serve immediately.
- Substitute 1/2 large package frozen shredded potatoes for the chopped or sliced potatoes if desired.

Nutritional Facts Per Serving: Cal 390, Fat 19g, Chol 180mg, Sod 790mg, Carbo 31g, Fiber 4g, Protein 23g, Vitamin A 10%, Vitamin C 6%, Calcium 10%, Iron 15%

SPICY RED RICE AND SAUSAGE

Three classic heartland ingredients—tomatoes, smoked sausage, and rice—combine to give this appealing main dish its sweet-spicy flavor and interesting texture.

SERVINGS
8

PREPARATION TIME
10 minutes

COOKING TIME
10 minutes

1 (14.5-ounce) can Red Gold® Diced Tomatoes & Green Chilies
8 ounces smoked sausage, sliced
1/2 cup red French salad dressing
1 medium green bell pepper, chopped
1 medium onion, chopped
Salt and pepper to taste
1 cup instant long grain white rice

 TREASURE IN THE FREEZER

Having some leftover Red Gold® Diced Tomatoes Roasted Garlic & Onion is never a problem. Seal the tomatoes in a freezer bag and freeze for up to three months. Then, thaw and use them to add a rich garlic, onion, and tomato flavor to soup, stew, or chili. Or heat the tomatoes with other vegetables as a side dish, toss them into pasta salad, or use the tomatoes to make salsa.

- Combine the undrained Red Gold® Diced Tomatoes & Green Chilies, sausage, salad dressing, green bell pepper, onion, salt and pepper in a large saucepan and mix well. Bring to a boil.
- Boil for 5 minutes, stirring occasionally. Stir in the rice and cover. Remove from heat. Let stand for 5 minutes. Fluff with a fork before serving.

Nutritional Facts Per Serving: Cal 220, Fat 14g, Chol 15mg, Sod 740mg, Carbo 20g, Fiber 1g, Protein 5g, Vitamin A 8%, Vitamin C 20%, Calcium 2%, Iron 8%

COLORFUL TACO BAKE

SERVINGS
6

PREPARATION TIME
10 minutes

BAKING TIME
30 minutes

Ready for a new dimension to the ever-popular taco? With this recipe you can prepare the recipe in the oven and apply your favorite topping just before eating.

1 pound ground beef

1 envelope taco seasoning mix

1 cup baking mix

1/3 cup cold water

1 cup (4 ounces) shredded Cheddar cheese

Red Gold® Diced Tomatoes, drained

CUT THOSE FAT GRAMS!

Ground beef can be very high in fat. Look for extra-lean ground beef, or try this technique for rinsing away some of the excess fat: After cooking the beef until it is no longer pink, blot it with paper towels and place it in a colander. Pour 4 cups of boiling water over the cooked beef; drain it well and use it as directed in the recipe.

- Preheat the oven to 450°F. Cook the ground beef and seasoning mix using package directions. Combine the baking mix and cold water in a bowl and mix until a soft dough forms. Pat the dough over the bottom of a greased 8×8-inch baking dish.
- Spread the ground beef mixture over the dough. Bake for 25 to 30 minutes or until a wooden pick inserted in the center comes out clean; do not overbake. Sprinkle with the cheese. Let stand for 1 to 2 minutes or until the cheese melts. Cut into 6 equal pieces. Serve with sour cream, shredded lettuce and Red Gold® Diced Tomatoes.
- **Note:** Use shredded taco-seasoned cheese and Red Gold® Diced Tomatoes Mexican Fiesta for even greater taco flavor.

Nutritional Facts Per Serving: Cal 360, Fat 21g, Chol 75mg, Sod 990mg, Carbo 20g, Fiber 1g, Protein 21g, Vitamin A 15%, Vitamin C 6%, Calcium 20%, Iron 15%

CHEESY BURGER MACARONI

SERVINGS
8

PREPARATION TIME
10 minutes

COOKING TIME
15 minutes

It's a fast and easy meal for the times when you've had a long day at work and not a lot of time at home. This recipe is used in several school lunch programs because children love it!

1 pound ground beef

1 cup chopped onion

1 (14.5-ounce) can Red Gold® Stewed Tomatoes

1 cup water

1 cup elbow macaroni

2 cups (8 ounces) shredded processed American cheese

USING THE MICROWAVE

Use a microwave to quickly cook ground beef, ground turkey, and ground sausage. Place meat in a plastic colander inside a microwave-safe shallow dish. Microwave for 1 minute, drain the shallow dish, and stir the meat. Continue this process until the meat is no longer pink. It will be drained and crumbled.

- Brown the ground beef with the onion in a skillet, stirring until the ground beef is crumbly and cooking until the onion is tender; drain. Stir in the undrained Red Gold® Stewed Tomatoes and water. Bring to a boil. Add the pasta and mix well.
- Bring to a boil; reduce the heat to low. Simmer for 10 minutes or until the pasta is tender, stirring occasionally. Sprinkle with the cheese and stir until melted.
- **Note:** No need to cook the macaroni in a separate pan. This recipe combines all the ingredients, including uncooked macaroni, in one skillet for easy preparation and cleanup.

Nutritional Facts Per Serving: Cal 280, Fat 16g, Chol 60mg, Sod 550mg, Carbo 16g, Fiber 1g, Protein 18g, Vitamin A 15%, Vitamin C 10%, Calcium 20%, Iron 10%

HAM AND TOMATO RICE SUPPER

This is a delicious twist to broccoli, rice, and cheese casserole and is VERY easy to prepare. With the addition of ham, the dish has added flavor and the complete meal is prepared in just one skillet.

SERVINGS
8

PREPARATION TIME
10 minutes

COOKING TIME
10 minutes

2 cups cooked ham strips

2 cups fresh broccoli florets

1 (14.5-ounce) can Red Gold® Diced Tomatoes Roasted Garlic & Onion

1 1/2 cups instant rice

8 ounces processed American cheese, cubed

- Combine the ham, broccoli and undrained Red Gold® Diced Tomatoes Roasted Garlic & Onion in a large skillet and mix well. Cook, covered, over medium heat for 3 minutes. Stir in the rice and cheese.
- Remove the skillet from the heat. Let stand, covered, for 7 minutes. Stir until the cheese melts. Serve with apple wedges.
- **Note:** Yields differ between regular rice and instant rice. One cup of uncooked regular rice equals 3 cups cooked, and 1 cup of instant rice equals 2 cups cooked. Instant rice must be used in this recipe because of the amount of liquid in the recipe and length of cooking time.

Nutritional Facts Per Serving: Cal 250, Fat 13g, Chol 45mg, Sod 860mg, Carbo 19g, Fiber 1g, Protein 15g, Vitamin A 20%, Vitamin C 30%, Calcium 20%, Iron 8%

 QUICK- AND EASY PARTNERS

To create an entrée in a flash, partner Red Gold® Diced Tomatoes Roasted Garlic & Onion, Red Gold® Diced Tomatoes Mexican Fiesta, or Red Gold® Diced Tomatoes Italian with broiled or grilled meats, such as chicken breasts, pork chops, fish steaks, or burgers.

EASY ONE-DISH MEAL

SERVINGS
6

PREPARATION TIME
10 minutes

COOKING TIME
10 minutes

Ground beef and potatoes take a tasty turn when teamed with Red Gold® Diced Tomatoes. This recipe will become a family favorite and a super way to start the week.

NEW CHOICE FOR PIZZA LOVERS

To make a tasty taco pizza, spread your favorite homemade or purchased pizza crust with Red Gold® Crushed Tomatoes with Green Pepper & Mushroom. Spoon refried beans over the tomatoes; then sprinkle on cooked ground beef or sausage and shredded cheese. Bake as directed on pizza crust package. Top the finished pizza with shredded lettuce and crushed tortilla chips for a tempting South-of-the-Border taste.

1 pound ground beef

2 (14.5-ounce) cans Red Gold® Diced Tomatoes Mexican Fiesta

1 (10.75-ounce) can cream of celery soup

1/2 cup water

1/2 cup Red Gold® Ketchup

1 tablespoon Worcestershire sauce

2 cups frozen hash brown potatoes

1 cup (4 ounces) shredded processed American cheese

- Brown the ground beef in an electric skillet, stirring until crumbly; drain. Stir in the undrained Red Gold® Diced Tomatoes Mexican Fiesta, soup, water, Red Gold® Ketchup and Worcestershire sauce. Bring to a boil, stirring occasionally. Stir in the hash brown potatoes. Reduce the heat to low.
- Cook, covered, for 10 minutes or until the potatoes are tender, stirring occasionally. Sprinkle with the cheese. Serve immediately.
- **Note:** To make shepherd pie, mix the frozen hash brown potatoes with a can of cream of celery soup and top the ground beef and vegetable mixture. Cook as directed above.

Nutritional Facts Per Serving: Cal 260, Fat 13g, Chol 50mg, Sod 750mg, Carbo 19g, Fiber 2g, Protein 15g, Vitamin A 20%, Vitamin C 10%, Calcium 10%, Iron 10%

HOT DOG MEDLEY

On the evenings when time to prepare dinner is fifteen minutes, this is the meal for you. With the help of canned products and your microwave, the family will have a complete meal in minutes.

SERVINGS
6

PREPARATION TIME
5 minutes

COOKING TIME
10 minutes

1 (15-ounce) can Red Gold® Chili Hot Beans
1 (14.5-ounce) can Red Gold® Diced Tomatoes Chili Ready with Onions
8 ounces fully cooked hot dogs, sliced crosswise
1 tablespoon prepared mustard
6 hamburger buns, split
1/2 cup (2 ounces) shredded Cheddar cheese

- Combine the Red Gold® Chili Hot Beans, undrained Red Gold® Diced Tomatoes Chili Ready with Onions, hot dogs and mustard in a 2-quart microwave-safe dish with cover and mix well. Microwave, covered, on High for 6 to 8 minutes; stir.
- Arrange the buns on a paper towel in the microwave. Microwave for 30 to 60 seconds or until warm. Arrange the buns cut side up on a serving plate.
- Spoon the chili mixture over the buns. Sprinkle with the cheese. Serve immediately.

Nutritional Facts Per Serving: Cal 370, Fat 16g, Chol 40mg, Sod 800mg, Carbo 41g, Fiber 5g, Protein 15g, Vitamin A 15%, Vitamin C 8%, Calcium 20%, Iron 20%

 FLAVORFUL LUNCHES

Cottage cheese will take on a whole new dimension when you top it with either Red Gold® Diced Tomatoes Italian or Red Gold® Diced Tomatoes Mexican Fiesta or use Red Gold® Diced Tomatoes Italian as the dressing on your favorite prepared salad. Complete the lunch with crackers and cheese.

NO-BAKE SALAD PIZZA

SERVINGS
10

PREPARATION TIME
10 minutes

For this recipe, use a ready-to-top prepared pizza crust because of the extra seasonings and cheese already baked into the crust. The spinach dip adds a unique flavor to this summer afternoon meal.

1 cup prepared spinach dip
1 (10-ounce) prebaked Italian pizza crust
1 cup chopped fresh broccoli
1 (6-ounce) package prepared chicken breast, chopped
2 (14.5-ounce) cans Red Gold® Diced Tomatoes, drained
1/4 cup sliced green onions
1/4 cup grated Parmesan cheese

BROCCOLI TRIVIA

Broccoli means "cabbage sprout" in Italian and is a cruciferous cousin of cabbage, brussels sprouts, and cauliflower. It was first cultivated in the United States in 1920. A head of broccoli is made of many clusters of small flower buds, or sprouts, called flowerets.

- Spread the spinach dip evenly over the pizza crust to within 1/2 inch of the edge. Top with the broccoli, chicken, Red Gold® Diced Tomatoes, green onions and cheese.
- Cut the pizza into wedges. Serve immediately.
- **Note:** Have you noticed the freshness dates on foods? A "sell by" date indicates when the product should be removed from grocery store shelves. It doesn't necessarily mean the food is spoiled. Often a food is good for up to one week after the posted "sell by" date. A "use by" date tells you when a product may go bad. If only one date appears on a food, assume it is a "use by" date.

Nutritional Facts Per Serving: Cal 270, Fat 14g, Chol 35mg, Sod 690mg, Carbo 23g, Fiber 1g, Protein 11g, Vitamin A 10%, Vitamin C 15%, Calcium 15%, Iron 8%

Our
VEGETABLE PATCH

SUMMERTIME CROSTINI

SERVINGS
16

PREPARATION TIME
20 minutes

BAKING TIME
9 minutes

Crostini, in Italian, refers to small toasted rounds of bread usually topped with a tomato and basil mixture. Vine-ripened Red Gold® Tomatoes and fresh basil make these crostini irresistible. It's a refreshing light appetizer or snack with a zesty fresh flavor.

32 (1/4-inch-thick) slices baguette-style French bread
1 (28-ounce) can Red Gold® Whole Peeled Tomatoes,
drained, finely chopped
1 (6-ounce) jar marinated artichoke hearts, drained, finely chopped
2 tablespoons chopped fresh basil
1/2 teaspoon salt
1/8 teaspoon coarsely ground pepper

TASTY TOMATO BRUSCHETTA

For a great appetizer or weekend afternoon snack, brush extra-virgin olive oil onto thick slices of sourdough or Italian bread and grill or toast. Combine one 14.5-ounce can drained, Red Gold® Diced Tomatoes Italian, 1/2 cup grated Parmesan cheese and 3 tablespoons chopped basil in a small bowl. Spoon the tomato mixture onto the grilled bread. Broil for 1 minute to melt the cheese.

- Preheat the oven to 325°F. Line a baking sheet with foil. Arrange the bread slices in a single layer on the prepared baking sheet. Spray the bread slices lightly with nonstick cooking spray. Bake for 6 to 9 minutes or until crisp. Remove the bread slices to a wire rack to cool.
- Combine the Red Gold® Whole Peeled Tomatoes, artichokes, basil, salt and pepper in a bowl and mix well.
- Spoon some of the tomato mixture onto each bread slice. Arrange the cooled crostini on a serving platter. Serve immediately.

Nutritional Facts Per Serving: Cal 80, Fat 1g, Chol 0mg, Sod 260mg, Carbo 14g, Fiber 1g, Protein 3g, Vitamin A 4%, Vitamin C 6%, Calcium 2%, Iron 4%

PESTO PINWHEELS

MAKES
16 pinwheels

PREPARATION TIME
15 minutes

BAKING TIME
17 minutes

These quick Italian-inspired appetizers are fabulous hors d'ouevre that ALWAYS get raves. And to think they only have three ingredients.

1 (8-count) can crescent rolls
1/3 cup commercially prepared basil pesto
1 (14.5-ounce) can Red Gold® Diced Tomatoes Italian, drained

PESTO

Pesto is an uncooked sauce made with fresh basil, garlic, pine nuts, Parmesan cheese, and olive oil. The ingredients can either be crushed with mortar and pestle or finely chopped with a food processor. This classic, fresh-tasting sauce originated in Genoa, Italy, and although used on a variety of dishes, it is a favorite with pasta.

- Preheat the oven to 350°F. Unroll the crescent roll dough into 2 large rectangles on a hard surface. Press the perforations to seal.
- Spread 1/2 of the pesto over the surface of each rectangle to within 1/4 inch of the edges. Sprinkle with the Red Gold® Diced Tomatoes Italian. Roll as for a jelly roll; pinch the edges to seal.
- Cut each roll into 8 slices. Arrange the slices cut side up on an ungreased baking sheet. Bake for 12 to 17 minutes or until light brown. Remove to a serving platter. Serve warm.

Nutritional Facts Per Pinwheel: Cal 100, Fat 6g, Chol 0mg, Sod 320mg, Carbo 11g, Fiber 0g, Protein 2g, Vitamin A 4%, Vitamin C 4%, Calcium 4%, Iron 4%

ARTICHOKE AND TOMATO DIP

SERVINGS
8

PREPARATION TIME
10 minutes

BAKING TIME
25 minutes

This dip is delicious hot, cold, or at room temperature. Serve with tortilla chips or pita wedges, and be sure to treat yourself to a few bites, as it does not last long at parties!

1 (14.5-ounce) can artichoke hearts, drained, chopped
1 1/2 cups (6 ounces) grated Parmesan cheese
1 cup fat-free mayonnaise
1 (14.5-ounce) can Red Gold® Diced Tomatoes, drained
1/2 cup sliced green onions

- Preheat the oven to 350°F. Combine the artichokes, cheese and mayonnaise in a bowl and mix well. Spoon into a 9-inch-oval baking dish.
- Bake for 20 to 25 minutes or until light brown. Top with the Red Gold® Diced Tomatoes and green onions.
- May prepare 1 day in advance and store, covered, in the refrigerator. Bake just before serving.

Nutritional Facts Per Serving: Cal 140, Fat 3.5g, Chol 10mg, Sod 610mg, Carbo 17g, Fiber 1g, Protein 7g, Vitamin A 4%, Vitamin C 6%, Calcium 15%, Iron 6%

 TOMATO PASTE TIP

Here is a slick way to quickly remove every rich, flavorful dab of Red Gold® Tomato Paste from the can. Using a can opener, open both ends of the can; then discard one end. Working over a bowl, use the other end to push against the paste to remove it easily and neatly from the can.

LAYERED MEXICAN DIP

SERVINGS
12

PREPARATION TIME
10 minutes

REFRIGERATION TIME
1 hour

Whether served as an appetizer before your meal, or as a snack in front of the TV, this colorful dip is sure to become a family favorite.

8 ounces cream cheese, softened

1 tablespoon taco seasoning mix

2 avocados, mashed

1 cup Red Gold® Salsa, or 1 (14.5-ounce) can Red Gold® Diced Tomatoes & Green Chilies

1 cup (4 ounces) shredded Cheddar cheese

1 cup shredded lettuce

1/2 cup chopped green onions

2 tablespoons sliced pitted black olives

STORING GREEN ONIONS

To store green onions, cut the roots and trim the green tops to fit into a jar. Rinse and dry completely. Cover and store in the jar in the refrigerator. The green onions will keep for weeks and won't get soft.

- Combine the cream cheese and seasoning mix in a bowl and mix well. Spread over the bottom of a 9-inch-round baking dish.
- Layer with the avocados, Red Gold® Salsa, cheese, lettuce, green onions and olives. Chill, covered, for 1 hour or longer. Serve with tortilla chips.

Nutritional Facts Per Serving: Cal 170, Fat 15g, Chol 30mg, Sod 370mg, Carbo 6g, Fiber 5g, Protein 5g, Vitamin A 15%, Vitamin C 8%, Calcium 8%, Iron 4%

TOMATO TART

When Fran Reichart, founder of Red Gold®, Inc., learned we were developing a cookbook, she asked to contribute a recipe. Fran always had a flair for using tomatoes in unique and interesting ways. This recipe combines the flavors of cheese, basil, and tomatoes in a delicate piecrust.

SERVINGS
12

PREPARATION TIME
20 minutes

BAKING TIME
40 minutes

1 unbaked (9-inch) pie shell
2 (14.5-ounce) cans Red Gold® Diced Tomatoes Roasted Garlic & Onion
1/2 cup fresh basil, chopped
1/4 teaspoon salt
1 cup (4 ounces) shredded Cheddar cheese
1 cup (4 ounces) shredded Swiss cheese
1/2 cup mayonnaise

TOMATO TOKEN

Performance and pride have always been an important part of the Red Gold® tradition. In the early years of the company, tomatoes were peeled by hand. Peelers were paid based on the number of buckets of tomatoes peeled. The peeler was given a "Tomato Token" for each bucket that was graded "Fancy" (no core, no peel, and no part of the tomato chopped off!). Additional money was paid for each token earned. Thus, the tokens became a valuable incentive for outstanding quality.

- Preheat the oven to 375°F. Fit the pie shell into a 9-inch pie plate. Prick the bottom of the pastry with a fork. Bake for 12 minutes.
- Combine the undrained Red Gold® Diced Tomatoes Roasted Garlic & Onion, basil and salt in a bowl and mix well. Spread the tomato mixture evenly in the prepared pie plate. Combine the Cheddar cheese, Swiss cheese and mayonnaise in a bowl and mix well. Spread evenly over the tomato mixture. Bake for 20 to 25 minutes or until light brown. Cut into bite-size pieces. Serve warm.
- **Note:** A tomato tart can be served as an appetizer or an entrée. Serve with a soup of your choice, tossed green salad and a raspberry ice for dessert.

Nutritional Facts Per Serving: Cal 230, Fat 18g, Chol 25mg, Sod 250mg, Carbo 12g, Fiber 1g, Protein 6g, Vitamin A 15%, Vitamin C 6%, Calcium 15%, Iron 4%

ITALIAN BEAN SOUP

SERVINGS
4

PREPARATION TIME
5 minutes

COOKING TIME
25 minutes

A hearty and healthy soup that is a favorite with friends and family. Try it! We're positive you'll be pleased. It keeps well and tastes even better the next day. Soup may be assembled in a slow cooker in the morning to be ready for supper when you get home from work.

1 (28-ounce) can Red Gold® Stewed Tomatoes, chopped

1 (16-ounce) package frozen vegetable combination of choice

1 (15-ounce) can vegetable broth

1 (15-ounce) can pinto beans

1 (15-ounce) can great northern beans

5 garlic cloves, finely chopped

1 teaspoon Italian seasoning

2 tablespoons pesto

- Combine the undrained Red Gold® Stewed Tomatoes, frozen vegetables, broth, undrained pinto beans, undrained Great Northern beans, garlic and Italian seasoning in a stockpot and mix well. Bring to a boil; reduce the heat to low.
- Simmer, covered, for 25 minutes, stirring occasionally. Stir in the pesto. Ladle into soup bowls. Serve with sesame breadsticks and spinach salad.
- **Note:** If you do not have Italian seasoning on hand, you can use 1/4 teaspoon each dried oregano, basil and thyme leaves.

Nutritional Facts Per Serving: Cal 280, Fat 4g, Chol 0mg, Sod 840mg, Carbo 49g, Fiber 10g, Protein 13g, Vitamin A 45%, Vitamin C 30%, Calcium 15%, Iron 25%

LOOK AT THE LABEL

Red Gold® has a new look! We talked to our customers and the results are in—you love the big red tomato, but you want to see each variety at a glance. So, we've added color-coded ribbons for all the flavors for easy shopping.

SPICY TOMATO BREAD

This tomato quick bread, full of spices, is bursting with flavor and is a joy to make and eat.

CREAMY TOMATO SOUP

Serve this old-fashioned and easy to prepare soup for a light lunch or dinner. Sauté 4 garlic cloves in 1 tablespoon vegetable oil in a saucepan until tender. Process the garlic and three 14.5-ounce cans undrained Red Gold® Stewed Tomatoes in a blender or food processor until smooth. Return the tomato mixture to the saucepan. Bring to a boil; reduce heat to low. Stir in 1 cup whipping cream. Simmer just until heated through, stirring occasionally. Ladle equal amounts into 6 soup bowls.

Makes 6 servings

^{1}/2 cup each sugar and packed brown sugar

^{1}/3 cup vegetable oil

2 eggs

1 (15-ounce) can Red Gold® Crushed Tomatoes

1^1/2 cups flour

1 teaspoon each cinnamon and baking soda

^{1}/2 teaspoon baking powder

^{1}/2 teaspoon each allspice, nutmeg and ground cloves

^{1}/4 teaspoon salt

^{1}/2 cup sliced almonds

- Preheat the oven to 350°F. Mix sugar, brown sugar, oil and eggs in a bowl. Stir in the Red Gold® Crushed Tomatoes.
- Combine the flour, cinnamon, baking soda, baking powder, allspice, nutmeg, cloves and salt in a bowl and mix well. Add to the tomato mixture and mix well; the batter will be thin.
- Pour the batter into a greased 9×5-inch loaf pan. Sprinkle with the almonds. Bake for 40 to 45 minutes or until a wooden pick inserted in the center comes out clean. Cool in pan for 10 minutes. Remove to a wire rack to cool completely before slicing.

Nutritional Facts Per Serving: Cal 180, Fat 8g, Chol 25mg, Sod 220mg, Carbo 25g, Fiber 1g, Protein 3g, Vitamin A 6%, Vitamin C 2%, Calcium 4%, Iron 8%

RED GOLD® CON QUESO

SERVINGS
16

PREPARATION TIME
5 minutes

COOKING TIME
7 minutes

This spicy appetizer is perfect for a last-minute party.
By using the microwave, you have it ready in just a few minutes.
Omit the spinach for a great spicy cheese dip.

1/2 (10-ounce) package frozen chopped spinach, thawed, drained
1 pound processed American cheese, cubed
1 (14.5-ounce) can Red Gold® Diced Tomatoes & Green Chilies, drained

- Press the excess moisture from the spinach. Combine the cheese and Red Gold® Diced Tomatoes & Green Chilies in a microwave-safe dish. Microwave on High for 2 minutes; stir. Microwave on High for 3 minutes longer or until the cheese melts. Stir in the spinach.
- Microwave on High for 2 minutes and stir. Serve with hot breadsticks, tortilla chips and/or assorted fresh vegetables.
- **Note:** To quickly thaw spinach, cut small slits in center of pouch. Microwave on High for 2 to 3 minutes. Remove spinach from pouch; squeeze dry with paper towel.

Nutritional Facts Per Serving: Cal 100, Fat 6g, Chol 25mg, Sod 490mg, Carbo 5g, Fiber 1g, Protein 6g, Vitamin A 30%, Vitamin C 4%, Calcium 20%, Iron 2%

JUICE
BOOST

Perk up the flavor of homemade soups, chilies, and stews by adding the juice you have drained from Red Gold® Diced Tomatoes or Red Gold® Whole Peeled Tomatoes. When a recipe calls for these products drained, freeze the juice in ice cube trays. Place the juice cubes in a resealable freezer bag and return the bag to the freezer. Then, as you simmer your soup or stew, just add an ice cube or two for a rich tomato flavor.

TOMATOES MOZZARELLA

SERVINGS
8

PREPARATION TIME
20 minutes

BAKING TIME
30 minutes

No food is more comforting than a hot and hearty fresh-from-the-oven casserole. This recipe uses bread and tomatoes to create a side dish rich in flavor and texture. All you do is toss the ingredients together and turn on the oven.

SIDE DISH PERFECTION

Simply warm the Red Gold® Crushed Tomatoes with Green Pepper & Mushroom, spoon it over hot cooked spaghetti or other pasta, and sprinkle with some grated Parmesan cheese or shredded mozzarella cheese. For variety, use corkscrew macaroni or wagon-wheel pasta and stir cooked whole kernel corn or mixed vegetables into the sauce before heating it.

1 (28-ounce) can Red Gold® Whole Peeled Tomatoes, drained, sliced

4 cups soft bread cubes

3 cups (12 ounces) shredded mozzarella cheese

4 slices crisp-cooked bacon, drained, crumbled

1/2 cup (1 stick) butter, melted

1/2 cup chopped celery

1/2 cup chopped onion

2 eggs, beaten

1/2 teaspoon garlic salt

1 tablespoon oregano

1 tablespoon basil

- Preheat the oven to 350°F. Cover the bottom of a greased 12×8-inch baking dish with a single layer of the Red Gold® Whole Peeled Tomatoes. Combine the bread cubes, 2 cups of the cheese, bacon, butter, celery, onion, eggs, garlic salt, oregano and basil in a bowl and mix well.
- Spoon the bread mixture over the tomatoes in the prepared dish. Top with the remaining tomatoes. Sprinkle with the remaining 1 cup cheese. Bake for 30 minutes or until heated through.
- **Note:** Fry 2 pounds or more of bacon at a time, drain the slices well, then freeze them in a freezer bag. The slices are easy to remove individually for sandwiches or to crumble in recipes.

Nutritional Facts Per Serving: Cal 340, Fat 27g, Chol 125mg, Sod 780mg, Carbo 11g, Fiber 2g, Protein 15g, Vitamin A 30%, Vitamin C 20%, Calcium 30%, Iron 10%

SOUTHWESTERN SALAD

SERVINGS
4

PREPARATION TIME
15 minutes

This colorful, simple salad is a great potluck dish, or it serves as a main dish with tortillas or corn bread. Adding black beans gives it substance, and the bell pepper and onion give it color and spice.

1 cup Thousand Island salad dressing

1/4 teaspoon coarsely ground pepper

2 (14.5-ounce) cans Red Gold® Diced Tomatoes Mexican Fiesta, drained

1 (15-ounce) can black beans, drained, rinsed

1 (10-ounce) package frozen corn, cooked, drained

1/2 cup red bell pepper strips

1/2 cup thinly sliced red onion, cut into quarters

1 package (12-ounce) mixed salad greens

- Combine the salad dressing and pepper in a bowl and mix well. Combine the Red Gold® Diced Tomatoes Mexican Fiesta, black beans, corn, red bell pepper and red onion in a bowl and mix well.
- Arrange the salad greens on a serving platter. Top with the tomato mixture. Serve with the dressing mixture.
- **Note:** Use your favorite fat-free salad dressing to reduce fat grams. Keep this salad in the refrigerator for a healthy snack.

Nutritional Facts Per Serving: Cal 220, Fat 12g, Chol 10mg, Sod 650mg, Carbo 26g, Fiber 4g, Protein 6g, Vitamin A 45%, Vitamin C 80%, Calcium 2%, Iron 10%

 THE GREAT DEBATE— FRUIT OR VEGETABLE?

The U.S. Supreme Court made a ruling in 1893 to make tomatoes a vegetable. The reason for the ruling was economic. Back in 1893, imported fruits were not taxed, but imported vegetables were. To reduce price competition from foreign farmers and farmers in the U.S., the Supreme Court ruled the tomato a vegetable. So is the tomato a fruit or a vegetable? Let's just call it a tomato and leave it at that.

HEARTY VEGETABLE CHILI

SERVINGS
6

PREPARATION TIME
5 minutes

COOKING TIME
10 minutes

*Great meatless dish that takes very little time to prepare.
Ideal for potlucks!*

2 (14.5-ounce) cans Red Gold® Diced Tomatoes Chili Ready with Onions
1 (15-ounce) can garbanzo beans, drained, rinsed
1 (15-ounce) can black beans, drained, rinsed
1 (10-ounce) package frozen corn
2 teaspoons chili powder

- Combine the undrained Red Gold® Diced Tomatoes Chili Ready with Onions, garbanzo beans, black beans, corn and chili powder in a large saucepan and mix well. Bring to a boil over medium-high heat. Reduce the heat to low.
- Simmer, covered, for 10 minutes or until of the desired consistency, stirring occasionally. Ladle into chili bowls.
- Garnish with sour cream and shredded cheese and add hot pepper sauce for zip. Serve with herbed toast.

Nutritional Facts Per Serving: Cal 200, Fat 2g, Chol 0mg, Sod 680mg, Carbo 44g, Fiber 9g, Protein 10g, Vitamin A 25%, Vitamin C 25%, Calcium 10%, Iron 20%

REICHART
SOUP

Brian Reichart, Red Gold President/CEO, wants to share this family favorite recipe with you. Enjoy!

*2 large cans chicken and rice
   soup, undiluted
1 (14.5 ounce) can Red Gold®
   Diced Tomatoes & Green
   Chilies
Corn chips*

Combine the chicken and rice soup and Red Gold® Diced Tomatoes & Green Chilies in a medium saucepan. Heat for 10 minutes. Spoon into a bowl and sprinkle top with corn chips.

QUICK GARDEN QUESADILLAS

SERVINGS
6

PREPARATION TIME
10 minutes

COOKING TIME
2 minutes

These Mexican treats are like thin-crust grilled cheese sandwiches with a South-of-the-Border attitude. We've heightened the taste—and slashed the calories and fat—by using vegetables and no meat.

1 (14.5-ounce) can Red Gold® Diced Tomatoes Mexican Fiesta, drained
1 (7-ounce) can whole kernel corn, drained
1/2 cup slivered zucchini
1/4 cup finely chopped red onion
6 (8-inch) flour tortillas
2 cups (8 ounces) shredded Mexican blend cheese
Salt and pepper to taste
Chopped fresh cilantro to taste

SAUCY POTATOES

Baked potatoes take on a whole new dimension when topped with one of the several Red Gold® Diced Tomato varieties. Choose any of the rich blends to turn a baked potato into a quick-and-easy one-dish meal. Prepare baked potatoes in the microwave oven in just 4 minutes, rotating after 2 minutes.

- Combine the Red Gold® Diced Tomatoes Mexican Fiesta, corn, zucchini and red onion in a bowl and mix well.
- Place 4 of the tortillas on a hard surface. Spread each of the tortillas with 1/4 of the tomato mixture and 1/4 of the cheese. Sprinkle with salt, pepper and cilantro. Stack to make two 2-layer tortillas. Top each stack with 1 of the remaining tortillas. Spray the tops lightly with nonstick cooking spray.
- Arrange the quesadillas on a microwave-safe plate lined with waxed paper. Microwave on High for 1 minute or until the cheese melts. Cut into wedges. Garnish with sour cream and guacamole. Serve immediately.
- **Note:** For the flavor without the fat, try using reduced-fat cheese blends. Tuck Red Gold® Salsa into the filling for a fat-free jolt of taste.

Nutritional Facts Per Serving: Cal 280, Fat 13g, Chol 30mg, Sod 670mg, Carbo 30g, Fiber 3g, Protein 12g, Vitamin A 15%, Vitamin C 10%, Calcium 20%, Iron 10%

VEGETABLE CALZONE

SERVINGS
12

PREPARATION TIME
10 minutes

BAKING TIME
30 minutes

Our version of the popular Italian-stuffed pizza features fresh vegetables, vine ripe Red Gold® tomatoes, and cheese. Cut into squares and serve for a nutritious lunch.

1 (10-ounce) can refrigerator pizza crust

1/2 cup Red Gold® Tomato Sauce

2 cups (8 ounces) shredded mozzarella cheese

1 (14.5-ounce) can Red Gold® Diced Tomatoes Roasted Garlic & Onion, drained

1 cup chopped assorted fresh vegetables, such as carrots, broccoli and celery

1/2 cup (2 ounces) grated Parmesan cheese

■ Preheat the oven to 375°F. Unroll the pizza dough onto a baking sheet. Pat into a 12×12-inch square. Spread the Red Gold® Tomato Sauce to within 1 inch of the edge on half the dough. Sprinkle with half the mozzarella cheese. Top with the Red Gold® Diced Tomatoes Roasted Garlic & Onion and fresh vegetables. Sprinkle with the remaining mozzarella cheese.

■ Reserve 1 tablespoon of the Parmesan cheese. Sprinkle the remaining Parmesan cheese over the mozzarella cheese. Fold the dough over the filling and seal the edges with a fork. Sprinkle the reserved Parmesan cheese over the top. Bake for 25 to 30 minutes or until golden brown. Let stand for 5 minutes before slicing.

Nutritional Facts Per Serving: Cal 240, Fat 8g, Chol 20mg, Sod 590mg, Carbo 27g, Fiber 2g, Protein 14g, Vitamin A 40%, Vitamin C 20%, Calcium 25%, Iron 10%

PERFECT PIZZA CRUST

The trick to an even pizza crust is pressing the dough out from the center. Press the dough gently from the middle to the edge of the pan, then carefully push the dough up the sides of the pan. For a perfect cheese-stuffed crust, seal the dough edge tightly over pieces of string cheese.

83

FETTUCCINI DELIGHT

SERVINGS
6

PREPARATION TIME
5 minutes

COOKING TIME
15 minutes

Tomatoes and basil together are a sure hit! Very flavorful. For cheese lovers, substitute a strong Brie cheese for the Parmesan; otherwise a medium blend will do. Great served warm or cold.

6 ounces fettuccini

2 (14.5-ounce) cans Red Gold® Diced Tomatoes Roasted Garlic & Onion or Red Gold® Diced Tomatoes Italian

1/4 cup fresh basil, chopped

1/2 cup (2 ounces) shaved Parmesan cheese

WANT MORE RED GOLD® RECIPES?

Visit the recipe section of the web site, www.redgold.com. It is updated every two weeks with new recipes and cooking tips. In addition to great new recipes, you will also find a complete listing of our products with links to recipes that use each product, history of Red Gold®, careers at Red Gold®, and more.

- Cook the pasta using package directions; drain. Pour the undrained Red Gold® Diced Tomatoes Roasted Garlic & Onion into a large skillet. Bring to a boil; reduce the heat to low.
- Simmer for 5 minutes or until thickened, stirring occasionally. Stir in the pasta and basil. Simmer just until heated through, stirring occasionally. Sprinkle each serving with Parmesan cheese before serving.

Nutritional Facts Per Serving: Cal 150, Fat 3g, Chol 30mg, Sod 120mg, Carbo 22g, Fiber 2g, Protein 7g, Vitamin A 20%, Vitamin C 10%, Calcium 10%, Iron 10%

FRESH TOMATO BASIL PIZZA

SERVINGS
12

PREPARATION TIME
10 minutes

BAKING TIME
15 minutes

Our CEO, Brian Reichart, says, "This is the Greatest Pizza in the World."

1 (10-ounce) can refrigerator pizza crust
2 cups (8 ounces) shredded mozzarella cheese
3/4 cup mayonnaise
1/4 cup grated Parmesan cheese
1 garlic clove, minced
2 (14.5-ounce) cans Red Gold® Diced Tomatoes, drained
1 green bell pepper, chopped
2 tablespoons chopped fresh basil

- Preheat the oven to 425°F. Lightly grease a 12-inch pizza pan or 13×9-inch baking pan. Unroll the pizza dough and place in the center of the pizza pan. Pat the dough gently from the middle to the edge of the pan and up the side.
- Combine 1 cup of the mozzarella cheese, mayonnaise, Parmesan cheese and garlic in a bowl and mix well. Spread the cheese mixture over the dough. Arrange the Red Gold® Diced Tomatoes in a single layer over the prepared layers. Sprinkle with the green bell pepper and the remaining 1 cup mozzarella cheese. Bake for 12 to 15 minutes or until the crust is golden brown. Sprinkle with the basil just before serving.

Nutritional Facts Per Serving: Cal 170, Fat 8g, Chol 15mg, Sod 370mg, Carbo 16g, Fiber 1g, Protein 8g, Vitamin A 6%, Vitamin C 10%, Calcium 15%, Iron 4%

KEEPING BASIL FRESH

Basil wilts so quickly, but it perks up if set in a bowl of cold water for 30 minutes. Blot the leaves dry and store them at room temperature in a sealable plastic bag. If basil is stored in the refrigerator, it turns black.

RECIPE LOVERS
Delight

NACHO POTATO SOUP

SERVINGS
8

PREPARATION TIME
10 minutes

COOKING TIME
18 minutes

Use a prepared box of au gratin potatoes for a simple and delicious recipe! Creamy and cheesy, with a kick! The soup is great as a leftover...if there is any left over.

1 (14.5-ounce) can whole kernel corn

1 (14.5-ounce) can Red Gold® Diced Tomatoes & Green Chilies

1 (5.25-ounce) package au gratin potatoes

2 cups water

2 cups milk

2 cups cubed processed American cheese

1/8 teaspoon hot pepper sauce

2 tablespoons chopped fresh parsley

- Combine the undrained corn, undrained Red Gold® Diced Tomatoes & Green Chilies, contents of the potato package and water in a large saucepan and mix well. Bring to a boil; reduce the heat to low.
- Simmer, covered, for 15 to 18 minutes or until the potatoes are tender, stirring occasionally. Stir in the milk, cheese and hot pepper sauce.
- Cook until the cheese melts, stirring constantly. Ladle into soup bowls. Sprinkle with the parsley.

Nutritional Facts Per Serving: Cal 230, Fat 11g, Chol 30mg, Sod 1030mg, Carbo 22g, Fiber 2g, Protein 11g, Vitamin A 15%, Vitamin C 8%, Calcium 30%, Iron 4%

 SWITCH AND GO

When a full schedule keeps you away from the kitchen, put your slow cooker to work. Before work, place chuck roast, sliced onions, sliced carrots, diced potatoes and Red Gold® Stewed Tomatoes in your slow cooker and turn on Low. When you get home, dinner is ready to serve.

CHEESY PIZZA SOUP

SERVINGS
8

PREPARATION TIME
20 minutes

COOKING TIME
20 minutes

Anyone who is a fan of pizza will love this soup. After an afternoon of playing in the snow, warm everyone's heart with this tasty soup.

8 ounces Italian sausage

1 1/4 cups chopped fresh mushrooms

1 onion, finely chopped

2 cups water

1 (15-ounce) can pizza sauce

1 (14.5-ounce) can Red Gold® Diced Tomatoes Mexican Fiesta

1 cup sliced pepperoni, chopped

1/4 teaspoon Italian seasoning

1/4 cup grated Parmesan cheese

- Sauté the sausage, mushrooms and onion in a large saucepan for 2 to 3 minutes or until the sausage is brown; drain. Stir in the water, pizza sauce, undrained Red Gold® Diced Tomatoes Mexican Fiesta, pepperoni and Italian seasoning. Bring to a boil; reduce the heat to low.
- Simmer, covered, for 20 minutes, stirring occasionally. Stir in the Parmesan cheese just before serving. Ladle into soup bowls. May garnish with shredded mozzarella cheese.
- **Note:** Ground beef can be substituted for the Italian sausage. Canned mushrooms work just as well as fresh and are certainly more convenient. The soup can also simmer all day in a slow cooker.

Nutritional Facts Per Serving: Cal 170, Fat 11g, Chol 30mg, Sod 790mg, Carbo 8g, Fiber 2g, Protein 9g, Vitamin A 10%, Vitamin C 15%, Calcium 10%, Iron 10%

SIMPLE CHICKEN PARMESAN

SERVINGS
8

PREPARATION TIME
20 minutes

BAKING TIME
25 minutes

Treat your family to good food with very little work. Even if you do not know the icebox from the breadbox, you can prepare this dish with confidence.

6 (4-ounce) boneless skinless chicken breasts
2 eggs, beaten
1 cup Italian-style bread crumbs
2 tablespoons vegetable oil
2 (15-ounce) cans Red Gold® Crushed Tomatoes
with Green Pepper & Mushroom
1 1/2 cups (6 ounces) shredded mozzarella cheese

HOMEMADE BREAD CRUMBS

In the baking section of your grocery store you can purchase Italian-style bread crumbs ready to use. However, here is a process to make your own bread crumbs. Soft bread crumbs are made from fresh or slightly stale bread. Tear the bread apart with a fork or use a blender or food processor to break it into fluffy crumbs. Pile gently into a measuring cup and do not pack. Dry bread crumbs may be purchased or made from very dry bread or zwieback crackers. Place in a plastic bag and crush with a rolling pin. Season if desired.

- Preheat the oven to 375°F. Dip the chicken in the eggs and coat with the bread crumbs. Heat the oil in a large skillet over medium-high heat. Brown the chicken on both sides in the hot oil; drain.
- Spread 1 can of the Red Gold® Crushed Tomatoes with Green Pepper & Mushroom in an 11×7-inch baking dish. Arrange the chicken over the tomatoes. Top with the remaining can of Red Gold® Crushed Tomatoes with Green Pepper & Mushroom. Sprinkle with the cheese.
- Bake for 25 minutes or until the chicken is cooked through. Garnish with fresh basil.

Nutritional Facts Per Serving: Cal 290, Fat 11g, Chol 110mg, Sod 810mg, Carbo 19g, Fiber 1g, Protein 28g, Vitamin A 15%, Vitamin C 25%, Calcium 20%, Iron 10%

CHICKEN AND DUMPLINGS

SERVINGS
8

PREPARATION TIME
10 minutes

COOKING TIME
18 minutes

This is such an easy recipe...you open the cans, stir the ingredients together, and drop the dumplings on top...so simple and so delicious. This dish blends savory chunks of chicken with the wonderful taste of diced tomatoes, chili hot beans, and corn.

CHICKEN BREAST SUPREME

Pour Red Gold® Diced Tomatoes Mexican Fiesta or Red Gold® Diced Tomatoes with Roasted Garlic & Onion on boneless and skinless chicken breasts, cover and bake for 1 hour at 350°F. Remove cover, sprinkle with mozzarella cheese and return to oven and bake for 5 minutes.

2 cups chopped cooked chicken
1 (14.5-ounce) can each Red Gold®
  Diced Tomatoes and Red Gold®
  Diced Tomatoes Roasted
  Garlic & Onion
1 (15-ounce) can Red Gold® Chili
  Hot Beans
1 (15-ounce) can whole kernel
  corn, drained

1 teaspoon salt
1 teaspoon chili powder
1/2 teaspoon pepper
1 1/2 cups reduced-fat baking mix
1/2 cup cornmeal
2/3 cup skim milk
1/4 cup sliced green onions
1/2 cup (2 ounces) shredded
  reduced-fat Cheddar cheese

- Combine the chicken, undrained Red Gold® Diced Tomatoes and undrained Red Gold® Diced Tomatoes Roasted Garlic & Onion in a Dutch oven and mix well. Bring to a boil; reduce the heat to low.
- Simmer, covered, for 5 minutes, stirring occasionally. Stir in the Red Gold® Chili Hot Beans, corn, salt, chili powder and pepper. Bring to a boil; reduce the heat to medium.
- Combine the baking mix and cornmeal in a bowl and mix well. Stir in the skim milk and green onions until mixed. Drop the cornmeal mixture by teaspoonfuls over the hot chicken mixture. Cook for 10 minutes. Sprinkle with the cheese. Cook, covered, for 3 minutes longer. Serve with a fresh green salad drizzled with oil and vinegar dressing.

Nutritional Facts Per Serving: Cal 280, Fat 4g, Chol 20mg, Sod 750mg, Carbo 42g, Fiber 5g, Protein 16g, Vitamin A 15%, Vitamin C 10%, Calcium 10%, Iron 15%

HARVEST CHICKEN STEW

SERVINGS
6

PREPARATION TIME
15 minutes

COOKING TIME
30 minutes

This is a sweet and savory stew made with sweet potatoes, chicken breasts, and tomatoes. The stew is healthy, hearty, and quick.

4 boneless skinless chicken breasts, cut into $1/2$-inch pieces
Garlic salt and pepper to taste
$1/2$ cup flour
2 tablespoons vegetable oil
2 cups chopped peeled sweet potatoes
1 cup chopped onion
1 (14.5-ounce) can Red Gold® Stewed Tomatoes
$3/4$ cup each chicken broth and apple juice
$1/2$ teaspoon dill weed

THE HISTORY OF OUR LABEL

In the early 1970s, Red Gold® introduced its own brand of tomato products. The label did not change again until 1992. The most recent package graphics were introduced in the summer of 2000. All cans of Red Gold® products now feature a delicious recipe, including a picture.

- Sprinkle the chicken on both sides with garlic salt and pepper. Place the flour in a sealable plastic bag. Add the chicken. Toss until coated.
- Heat the oil in a large skillet. Cook the chicken in the hot oil until brown on both sides, turning once or twice. Remove the chicken to a platter with a slotted spoon, reserving the pan drippings.
- Sauté the sweet potatoes and onion in the reserved pan drippings until the onion is tender. Return the chicken to the skillet. Stir in the undrained Red Gold® Stewed Tomatoes, broth, apple juice and dill weed to the skillet. Bring to a boil; reduce the heat to low. Simmer for 25 to 30 minutes or until the chicken is cooked through, stirring frequently.

Nutritional Facts Per Serving: Cal 270, Fat 8g, Chol 50mg, Sod 280mg, Carbo 28g, Fiber 2g, Protein 23g, Vitamin A 8%, Vitamin C 50%, Calcium 4%, Iron 15%

TURKEY CRESCENT BRAID

SERVINGS
8

PREPARATION TIME
15 minutes

BAKING TIME
30 minutes

Prepare this beautiful recipe during the holiday season. With a small amount of effort on your part, you will be the talk of the party.

1/4 cup cream cheese with chives and onion, softened

1/4 cup sour cream with roasted garlic

1 (14.5-ounce) can Red Gold® Diced Tomatoes Roasted Garlic & Onion, drained

1 3/4 cups (about 8 ounces) cooked turkey breast strips

1 cup (4 ounces) shredded Italian blend cheese

1 (8-count) can crescent rolls

1 egg, beaten

1/2 cup sliced almonds

CRESCENT ROLL DOUGH

When working with refrigerated crescent rolls, keep the dough chilled until ready to use. After the dough is removed from the can, work quickly to be sure the rolls rise and brown evenly.

- Preheat the oven to 350°F. Combine the cream cheese and sour cream in a bowl and mix well. Stir in the Red Gold® Diced Tomatoes Roasted Garlic & Onion, turkey and cheese.
- Unroll the roll dough into 2 rectangles on a lightly greased baking sheet. Overlap the long sides of the rectangles to form a 14×9-inch rectangle; press the edges and perforations to seal. Spread the turkey mixture down the center of the rectangle, making a 3-inch-wide strip.
- Using scissors, make cuts at 1-inch intervals on the long sides of the dough to within 1/2 inch of the filling. Fold the strips alternately across the filling. Brush with the egg and sprinkle with the almonds. Bake for 28 to 30 minutes or until golden brown. Let stand for 5 minutes. Cut into crosswise slices. Serve with fresh fruit salad.

Nutritional Facts Per Serving: Cal 210, Fat 14g, Chol 70mg, Sod 200mg, Carbo 7g, Fiber 2g, Protein 15g, Vitamin A 10%, Vitamin C 4%, Calcium 15%, Iron 8%

INDEX